GIAN CARLO MENOTTI

Five Songs

for
Voice and Piano

ED 3596
ISBN 0-634-01706-3

G. SCHIRMER, Inc.

DISTRIBUTED BY

HAL•LEONARD®
CORPORATION
7777 W. BLUEMOUND RD. P.O. BOX 13819 MILWAUKEE, WI 53213

FIVE SONGS

FIVE SONGS

1. The Eternal Prisoner

(Texts by the composer)

Gian Carlo Menotti

pochissimo meno mosso

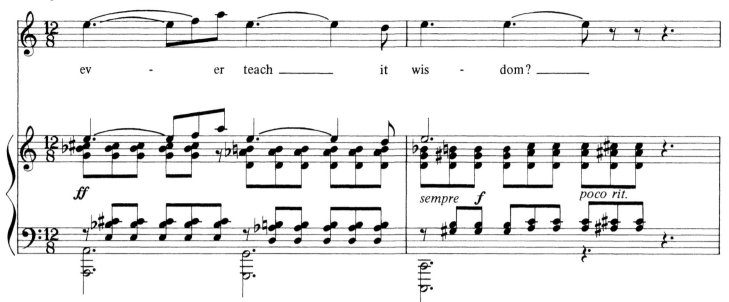

ev - er teach _____ it wis - dom? _____

Nev - er a - gain, _____ one

says; Then _____ de - lib - er - ate - ly un -

poco rall.

locks _____ the tor - ture cham - ber and

poco meno mosso

smiles _____ at ___ the ex - e - cu - tion - er.

mf ma pesante

Tempo I

2. The Idle Gift

Gian Carlo Menotti

I love what must be searched as well as read' - ly

of - fered, if joy _____ or pain ac -

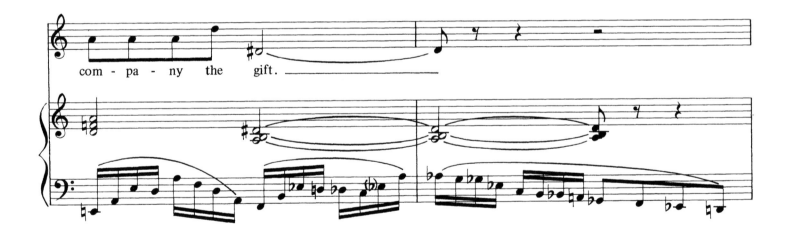

com - pa - ny the gift. _____

Your eas - y words and

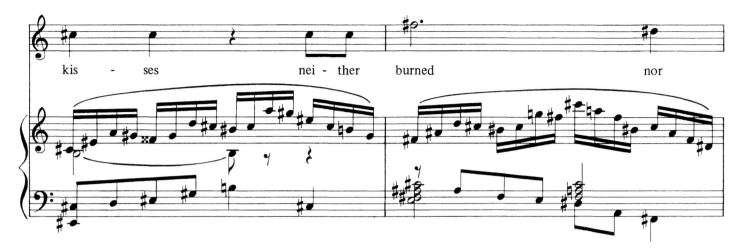

kis - ses   nei - ther   burned   nor

stung.

You left me   at   dawn   on a   dream - less   bed.

p   *a tempo*   *poco rit.*

3. The Longest Wait

Gian Carlo Menotti

Adagio, ma non troppo

No, _____ it is not love that I de-

sire, But _____ on-ly an an-swer to my

love; _____ A kiss of peace that bears no

Allegro moderato

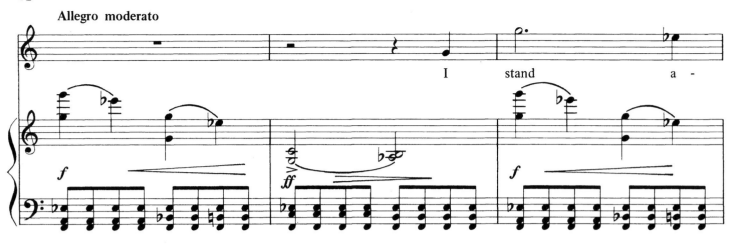

I stand a-

lone by storm - - - - y

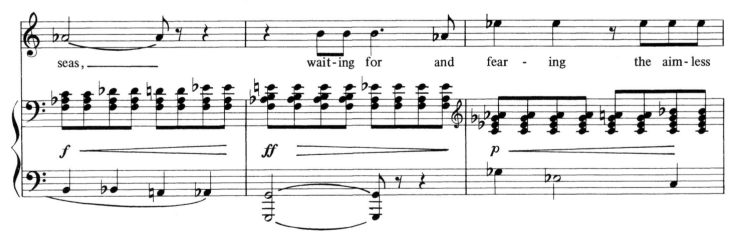

seas, waiting for and fear-ing the aim-less

poco rall.

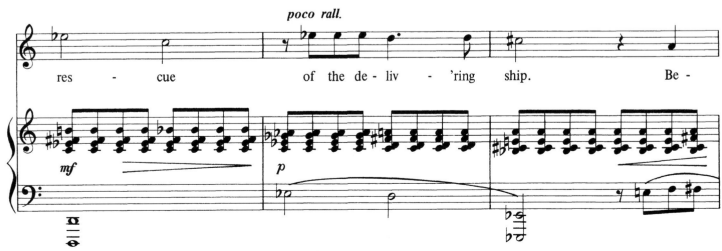

res - cue of the de-liv - 'ring ship. Be -

poco rall. *poco meno mosso*

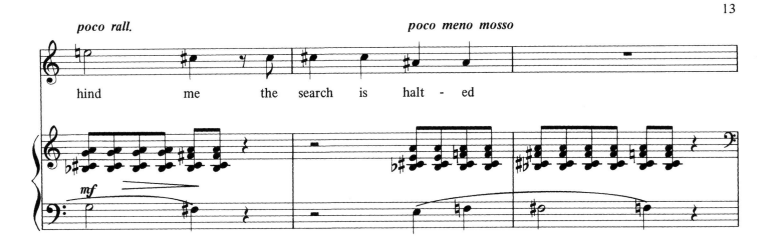

hind me the search is halt - ed

rall. molto *a tempo*

in the dark'n - ing for - est.

poco rall. *poco rall.*

All calls and cries are si - lenced.

Andante calmo

No,_____ I shall not ev - er tread a -

gain_____ the tor-tu-ous path ___ of my mis - takes. _____

poco rit.

Here I stand _____ scan - ning the sky _____

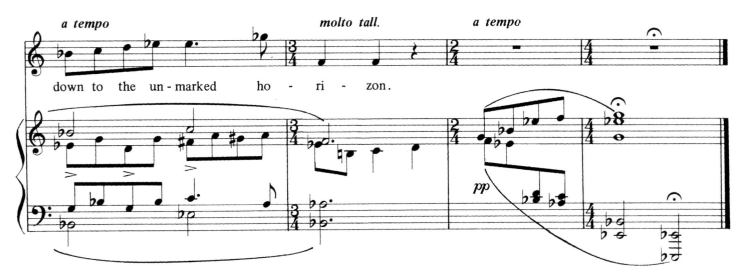

a tempo   *molto rall.*   *a tempo*

down to the un - marked ho - ri - zon.

4. My Ghost

Gian Carlo Menotti

Andante, molto moderato (with humor)

Oh yes, I too have a ghost in my home; But mine is a friend-ly ghost. It does-n't fright-en me; not my cat, nor my dog.

I can-not tell what its sex is for it wears a dirt-y

sheet as chil-dren do on Hal-low-een.

Like all ghosts

it fan-cies creak-y doors and wind-y

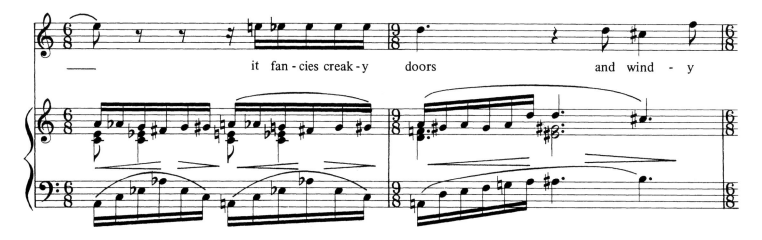

nights.   Some - times   be - hind my bed - room door

it sounds as if it were drag - ging heav - y chains, ____ Some-times it

Allegretto moderato

sighs. ____ But once it ap - pears in - side my room ____

(freely)

it stands there   not quite know - ing what to do,

rall.

f pesante

mf espress.

colla voce

and stares at me rath-er em-bar-as-sed-ly.

Once I asked why it wan-dered so aim-less-ly be-tween

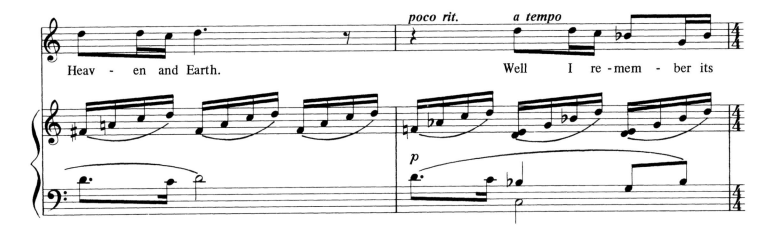

Heav- en and Earth. Well I re-mem- ber its

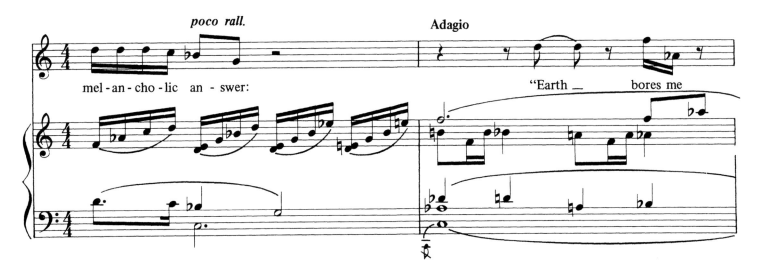

mel-an-cho-lic an-swer: "Earth __ bores me

Tempo I

poco rit.

but Heav - en fright - ens me." A jol - ly ghost in -

a tempo

deed! How - ev - er, it nev - er smiles. Af - ter all

poco rall. a tempo

death is a se - ri - ous thing.

Presto

5. The Swing

Gian Carlo Menotti

light _____ to cap - ture short - lived joy _____

f   *colla voce*   *ff* *a tempo*   *p*

— and then a - gain ___ the anx - ious plunge _____ in - to the wait - ing

void. _____

Don't be ap-pre -

pp

poco rit.

hen - sive. The game holds no sur - prise.

a tempo

Have you _____ not al - ways known it must come to an

end? There soon will be no wait - ing

poco rit.

arms to push you up a - gain.

The ropes are worn; the i - ron rings with

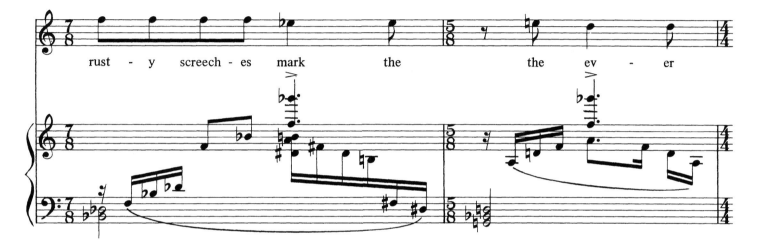

rust - y screech - es mark the the ev - er

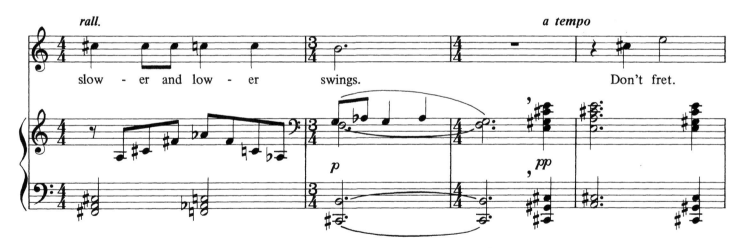

slow - er and low - er swings. Don't fret.

Don't move. Let it at last come to the fi - nal stop.

And turn your face a - way

from the de - cep - tive sky

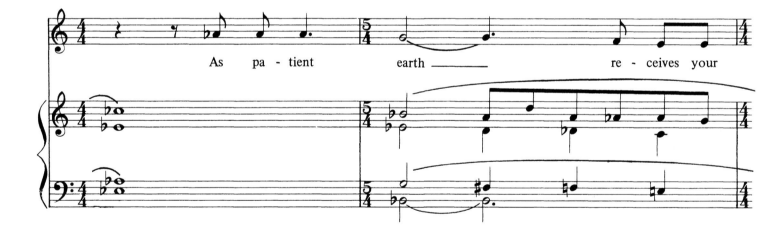

As pa - tient earth _____ re - ceives your

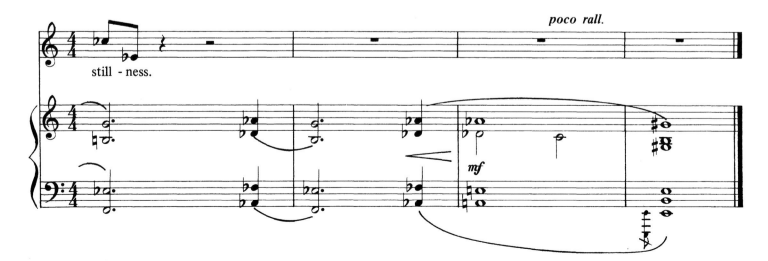

still - ness.